Friederike Sternberg

The King with the Cold Heart

Bibliographical Information of the Deutsche Nationalbibliothek:
This publication is listed in the Deutsche Nationalbibliographie
of the Deutsche Nationalbibliothek; detailed bibliographical
information can be accessed under http://dnb.dnb.de

Illustrations:
Elettra Francesca Cudignotto

Publishing:
BoD · Books on Demand GmbH,
Überseering 33, 22297 Hamburg, bod@bod.de

Printing:
Libri Plureos GmbH,
Friedensallee 273, 22763 Hamburg

ISBN: 978-3-7693-1352-9

FRIEDERIKE STERNBERG

THE KING
with the Cold Heart

Idea, concept and realization
by **Friederike Sternberg**

Illustrations by
Francesca Cudignotto

FOREWORD

Children growing up with a narcissistic parent often struggle for a lifetime with the toxic influences of their childhood. In my practice, I support children, adolescents, and adults in their journey towards greater self-confidence, assertiveness, and independence.

What children need most in a parental relationship - being seen with love, understanding, and reflection in the eyes of an adult - is something a narcissistic parent cannot adequately provide. To these parents, children are mainly an extension of themselves, fulfilling their own needs. Such experiences of not being truly acknowledged can leave deep marks on a child's soul.

These children are often confused and insecure, sometimes even angry and frustrated. Their gut feeling tells them that something is wrong and it is difficult for them to put this into words. The underlying issue is an internal conflict: the children love this parent but simultaneously feel disregarded and ignored by them. Most children blame themselves and therefore find it difficult to develop a healthy sense of self-worth. In cases of separation, they may also face the risk of losing a stable relationship as one parent attempts to alienate them from the other.

To gradually articulate, understand, and process the feelings and experiences shaping their development, these children need our support.

This book presents the topic of narcissism in a child-friendly manner using a metaphorical, fairy-tale-like narrative. It can help affected children confirm their gut feelings and find words for their emotions. It can also assist parents and therapists in discussing these topics with children and guiding them on their journey.

Jan Steinitz
Diploma Psychologist

Once upon a time, there was a king. His name was Ego. To be precise, Ego the Great.

He lived and ruled in his kingdom, reigning over all the people who lived there. The kingdom was a cold and uncomfortable place because Ego the Great had a cold heart. Every day, the people could feel its freezing coldness.

One of them was Flo. Flo was eight years old and lived with his mother and younger brother. They led a peaceful life, but it wasn't always easy.

"I'm so cold, I can't fall asleep. Can we light a fire, Mama?" Flo asked almost every evening.

"We have no more wood, dear, ever since Ego keeps everything for himself," his mother replied.

Flo thought for a moment and said, "I must do something. Just lying here and freezing won't change anything. Tomorrow, I will go to Ego and ask for help."

"What will you say to him?" asked his little brother from under their shared blanket.

"I'll tell him that we need wood to make a warm fire. He has plenty of wood in his castle - all the trees we cut down before winter are there.

He is our king, and surely, he wants us to be well. I'm sure he will say yes."

The next morning, Flo went to the castle. Ego the Great listened to Flo and promised,

"I will give you wood. My servants will bring it to you later."

Flo happily skipped back home to his family. "Mama, he will send us wood. Soon we won't be cold anymore," Flo rejoiced.

But nothing happened, for as so often before. Ego's words were empty and once again, he broke his promise. Flo and his family felt unheard and unimportant. Their hearts slowly started to grow colder.

Flo's family often suffered from great hunger. When it became unbearable, and they could barely sleep from hunger pains, Flo decided to go back to Ego the Great and ask for help again.

He wished that Ego the Great would listen to him, understand him and really help him this time." Ego, we need food, and you can give us some. After all, you are the king and have plenty of exquisite food in your castle. Do you want my family to starve?" Flo asked, frustrated.

Ego the Great listened and promised, "I will send you more food than you have ever seen. I will even prepare it myself, for I am the best cook far and wide." Then he laughed a loud, booming laugh.

Flo was delighted and skipped back home, believing Ego's words and that this time he was telling the truth. But soon, he realized that once again, nothing happened. As always, for the king words and deeds were two different things that do not belong together. Slowly, Flo began to understand that Ego the Great never kept his promises. Flo, his little brother, and their mother felt unloved and unimportant. Their hearts grew even colder.

Sometimes, Ego invited people from the village to his castle, telling them most fantastic, funny, and exciting stories. In all his stories, Ego the Great was the hero, but none of them were true.

Ego the Great was never honest. He loved to rule and he enjoyed being in complete control. This made him feel important and powerful. Every day he invented new rules and laws. These only applied to the people in his kingdom. Ego himself never followed them. Others were punished, but he could do whatever he wanted. Rules did not apply to him.

This made Flo and the other people angry, and their hearts became even colder.

Cold hearts do not feel good.

Flo was furious. No one should be treated this way or have their feelings ignored.

He and his brother lay awake, shivering from hunger and cold, whispering under their blanket about what to do.

"We must try to talk to the king again," said Flo.

"But then he will just get angry and loud again," his brother said fearfully.

"We can do this. If we stick together, we are strong."

he two went to the castle. The guards would not let them in. Flo had prepared for this situation and so he distracted them with a trick.

When the brothers finally stood before the king, he roared, "Who let you gnomes in?" and looking at Flo: "Do you need backup because you are too afraid to face me alone?"

He laughed so loudly that Flo looked down, humiliated, and swallowed a big lump in his throat.

Still, Flo summoned all his courage and spoke honestly about why they had come. "We are so disappointed and feel left alone by you. Every time we ask for help, you promise, but never keep your word."

Ego the Great did not look at them while they spoke. It was as if they weren't even there. Then he started laughing again, but this time, it was hollow and forced. His eyes remained cold and lifeless.

Ego sneered, "It's your own fault that you are hungry and cold. Your mother should stop telling you lies and work harder. I already do so much for you, and yet you always want more. I can't help you. Now leave."

As they were about to leave, he shouted after them, "If you ever ask me for anything again, I will have you and your mother punished!"

Once again, Flo and his family felt unfairly treated, unloved, disappointed and sad.

Flo asked himself silently: "Why do we have a king if he doesn't do anything good for us? A king should love the people in his kingdom and not treat them like worthless objects!"

"He can only be a king because we exist," Flo said to his little brother as they lay in bed together again. His brother just nodded and was very quiet, then he said: "Ego the Great is a king with a cold heart. We are only important to him so that he can feel big and powerful and so that he is not alone. He doesn't really care about us."

And they both felt their hearts grow colder and colder.

The next morning, they made a decision with their mother. "We don't want to live another day in the kingdom of Ego the Great," said Flo, more certain than he had ever been in his life. "Yes, I feel the same way," his mother said. "I want to go with you to a place where there is a loving king who protects us, listens to us, is there for us and understands us - to a place that will warm our hearts again." Then she lovingly took her two sons in her arms. They packed their things as quickly as they could and left the kingdom for good. With every step they took away, they felt lighter and more liberated.

They found a place where warmth and love reigned - a kingdom ruled by Empathius. "Hello, my dears. We still have room and a hut for you," he greeted them warmly. He always treated the people in his kingdom kindly and honestly. King Empathius looked after them, listened to them and took their every wish and need seriously.

He was a kind and understanding king. Flo felt seen and loved. King Empathius took care of them, gave them food and drink and made sure they were never cold.

He did this of his own accord because he liked each of them and wanted everyone in his kingdom to be well. Empathius liked everyone for who they were. No one had to pretend and try to please him. He never got loud and angry.

The best moments were when King Empathius laughed. His laughter sounded genuine and warm. His eyes always shone, looked radiant and warmly loving. He always kept his promises.

From then on, Flo and his brother fell asleep happy and content every night.

FURTHER INFORMATION

These resources offer valuable insights, support, and guidance for those affected by narcissism.

Podcasts

Navigating Narcissism with Dr. Ramani – clinical psychologist Dr. Ramani Durvasula discusses manipulation, control, and healing from narcissistic relationships

Narcissist Apocalypse – personal stories from survivors of narcissistic abuse

The Covert Narcissism Podcast – focuses on recognizing and healing from covert narcissism

Waking Up to Narcissism – therapist Tony Overbay discussing ways to recognize and cope with narcissistic behaviors

Negotiate Your Best Life Podcast with Rebecca Zung – provides strategies for dealing with narcissists and reclaiming personal power

Books

Should I Stay or Should I Go:
Surviving a Relationship with a Narcissist
Dr. Ramani Durvasula

The Culture of Narcissism
Christopher Lasch

The Analysis of the Self
Heinz Kohut

Don't You Know Who I Am?:
How to Stay Sane in an Era of Narcissism,
Entitlement, and Incivility
Dr. Ramani Durvasula

The Covert Passive-Aggressive Narcissist
Debbie Mirza